THE DARK HISTORY OF
ANCIENT GREECE

THE DARK HISTORY OF
ANCIENT GREECE

Sean Callery

 Marshall Cavendish
Benchmark
New York

Website: www.marshallcavendish.us

This publication represents the opinions and views of the author based on Sean Callery's personal experience, knowledge, and research. The information in this book serves as a general guide only. The author and publisher have used their best efforts in preparing this book and disclaim liability rising directly and indirectly from the use and application of this book.

Other Marshall Cavendish Offices:
Marshall Cavendish International (Asia) Private Limited, 1 New Industrial Road, Singapore 536196 • Marshall Cavendish International (Thailand) Co Ltd. 253 Asoke, 12th Flr, Sukhumvit 21 Road, Klongtoey Nua, Wattana, Bangkok 10110, Thailand • Marshall Cavendish (Malaysia) Sdn Bhd, Times Subang, Lot 46, Subang Hi-Tech Industrial Park, Batu Tiga, 40000 Shah Alam, Selangor Darul Ehsan, Malaysia

Marshall Cavendish is a trademark of Times Publishing Limited

All websites were available and accurate when this book was sent to press.

Library of Congress Cataloging-in-Publication Data

Callery, Sean.
  The dark history of ancient Greece / by Sean Callery.
    p. cm.— (Dark histories)
  Summary: "A collection of dark deeds from Ancient Greece"—Provided by publisher.
  Includes bibliographical references and index.
  ISBN 978-1-60870-083-7
  1. Greece—History—To 146 B.C.—Juvenile literature. I. Title.
  DF215.C27 2010
  938—dc22
                          2009048379

Editorial and design by
Amber Books Ltd
Bradley's Close Close
74–77 White Lion Street
London N1 9PF
United Kingdom
www.amberbooks.co.uk

Project Editor: Sarah Uttridge
Design: Andrew Easton
Picture Research: Terry Forshaw and Natascha Spargo

PICTURE CREDITS:

FRONT COVER
bottom left, the temple of Hephaistos, courtesy of Toon Possemiers/iStockphoto; bottom right, a bust of Dionysus, courtesy of Photos.com; top, a Laconian black-figure cup depicting a warrior attacking a snake, courtesy of Peter Willi/Bridgeman Art Library

BACK COVER
The battle of Salamis, courtesy of Bettmann/Corbis

AKG Images: 3 (Peter Connolly), 19, 33b (Peter Connolly), 40 (Peter Connolly), 43, 52 (Rabatti Domingie); Alamy: 17b (Interfoto), 22 (Interfoto), 44 (North Wind Picture Archives); Art Archive: 8 (H.M. Herget/NGS Image Collection), 41 (H.M. Herget/NGS Image Collection), 54 (Alfredo Dagli Orti/Musée des Beaux Arts, Orléans); Bridgeman Art Library: 10 (Ashmolean Museum, University of Oxford), 16 (Acropolis Museum, Athens), 30b, 32 (Boltin Picture Library); Corbis: 9 (Bettmann), 17t (Hoberman Collection), 25 (Francis G. Mayer), 28 (Stapleton Collection), 36 (Bettmann), 38 (Hulton-Deutsch Collection), 42 (Bettmann); De Agostini Picture Library: 29, 30t (G. Nimatallah), 57 (G. Dagli Orti); Dreamstime: 59 (Valery Shanin); Fotolia: 6 (Dino Hrustanovic), 11 (Paul Picone), 49 (Antony McAulay), 51 (Mrakor); Getty Images: 13 (SuperStock), 14 (Bridgeman Art Library), 20 (Time & Life Pictures), 23 (Hulton Archive), 34 (National Geographic); Mary Evans Picture Library: 26 (Edwin Wallace), 33t, 47, 50, 55, 56 (Edwin Wallace) Marie-Lan Nguyen: 18, 46, 58; Photos 12: 48 (ARJ); Photos.com: 2/3, 24; Photoshot: 31 (World Illustrated); Public Domain: 35; TopFoto: 12 (Granger Collection), 39 (Granger Collection)

Printed in China

135642

Contents

Chapter 1

Silver and Slaves

Greece was home to one of the great ancient **civilizations**. It was a place of **democracy**, notable thinkers, amazing inventions, huge advances in medicine, and classical architecture. Even today we still use many ancient Greek ideas and designs.

Ancient Greek civilization began developing in the eighth century BCE. A group of **city-states** grew around the coast of the Mediterranean and Black seas. **Colonies** as far away as Spain, along the western coast of Asia, and from North Africa to the Black Sea were established as well. Ancient Greece and its colonies covered a far greater area than modern-day Greece. The leading city of ancient Greece was Athens, which became a democracy in 510 BCE.

The Parthenon still stands high above the city of Athens more than 2,400 years after it was built. This temple to the goddess Athena is a symbol of ancient Greek civilization.

Good for Some

Ancient Greece was a fantastic place to live if you were a wealthy man. However, this was not the case for the rest of society. Women and the poor were not allowed to vote. Neither were the group of people who did most of the work: **slaves**. Historians established that up to half of the population, or 100,000 people, of Athens were slaves. Another 20,000 slaves labored in the silver mines outside of the city.

Athens was the birthplace of democracy, but only male citizens over the age of twenty-one could vote.

Human Trade

Slaves were everywhere in ancient Greece. They had no rights and were traded in the market and at auctions. In 415 BCE slave owners paid 240 **drachmas** for a man, 165 drachmas for a woman, and 72 drachmas for a child. A drachma was roughly what most people earned in a day.

The average household had at least one slave. The wealthy owned two or three, but the most rich owned ten to twenty slaves. At one time, Nicias was the richest man in Athens. He owned one thousand slaves. He became even richer by renting them out to his fellow citizens.

Most slaves were brought in from outer regions and sold at markets. Prices depended on their skills and physical appearance.

Slave Targets

Young members of ancient Greek society were known to treat slaves badly. There is the story of young Ktesias who teamed up with his brother to make a game of emptying the contents of their **chamber pots** out of the window and onto the heads of slaves passing in the street.

Captives and Debtors

The majority of slaves were not born in Greece but were from other countries. Many were prisoners of war. Others were stolen from their villages and later sold. However, some poor Greeks who could not pay their debts had to become slaves to repay their creditors. A family in financial trouble might sell off a child or two into slavery to raise money.

Slaves were easy to identify. Most slaves had shaved heads while most free men had beards and mustaches. No age was considered too young to be a slave. As soon as a child was physically able to work, he or she could become a slave. One story tells of Epaphroditos, who was a slave by eight years old. As he leaned out of a window to escape his work and enjoy the sound of the musicians playing in the street, he fell out and plunged to his death.

No Rights

Owners were entitled to punish slaves who displeased them. The most common punishments were flogging or starving them of food.

Most of the slaves in ancient Greece lived a harsh life. Slaves were often chained together to stop them from escaping, as seen in this sculpture.

Slaves who ran away would be branded with a hot iron. The scar left on their skin would always reveal the fact that they had attempted to escape. By law, slaves were not supposed to be badly treated. If they were, however, they had no rights and could not take their case to court to seek justice. They weren't even allowed to give evidence in court for anyone else unless they had been tortured first to ensure they would tell the truth. Typical tortures were beatings, being stretched on a rack, and having vinegar poured up the nose.

Some slaves were treated very well and were even allowed to earn money running a business, provided they paid their owners a share of the profits. Slaves with management skills were highly paid and valued. One of Nicias's slaves had an important job that earned him a great deal of money. This slave was in charge of the thousands of slaves who worked in the silver mines.

Little Justice

It was very hard for ordinary citizens to receive justice, and impossible for slaves. If someone was robbed, there was no police. It was up to the victim to catch the criminal and bring him to court. If the victim couldn't do this, a magistrate could make the arrest. However, the victim had to be absolutely sure of the robber's identity. There was a fine of 1,000 drachmas for causing the wrong person to be arrested.

Treasure Chest

Ancient Greek society was one that supported the quest for knowledge. It takes a lot of money to pay for a society in which people have the time to think and develop new ideas instead of working all day. How did the Greeks manage this? The answer is silver. They were lucky enough

Slave craftsmen worked with the silver mined from the quarries to create coins such as this one, depicting the goddess Athena.

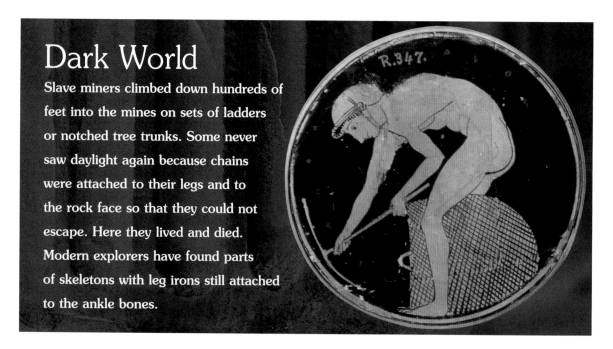

Dark World

Slave miners climbed down hundreds of feet into the mines on sets of ladders or notched tree trunks. Some never saw daylight again because chains were attached to their legs and to the rock face so that they could not escape. Here they lived and died. Modern explorers have found parts of skeletons with leg irons still attached to the ankle bones.

to find a huge amount of this valuable precious metal at the Laurion mines 25 miles (40 kilometers) southeast of Athens. The mines funded their lifestyle and were run on slave labor.

About two thousand shafts were dug as deep as 300 feet (91 meters) below the surface, linked together by a series of narrow underground tunnels. It was dangerous work chipping out the rock by the dim light of a candle. Slaves who didn't get injured usually only survived for three or four years before the lead in the silver ore poisoned them. Those who worked at the surface had the backbreaking job of smashing up the rock to extract the silver ore. About one-quarter of the slave miners of Laurion died every year.

City Life

The slaves in Athens who kept daily life running smoothly were much luckier than those who worked in the mines. Even so, life in an ancient Greek city was dirty, smelly, and dangerous. City streets were not laid out carefully, they were irregular, and were often piled high with stinking garbage.

Dirty Water

Sanitation was terrible in ancient Greece. Drinking water came from public fountains and was often dirty. It is believed that the lack of clean water was one of the major causes of death in ancient Greece. Historians believe that the average lifespan of an ancient Greek was about thirty years, less than half what it is in most developed countries today.

Plagues struck a number of city-states throughout the ancient world, killing a large part of the population. They were often caused by poor sanitation.

There were no hospitals or medical treatments for the sick. When large-scale diseases such as **typhus** or the **plague** struck, the Greeks asked priests to purify the air and ground. They used saltwater and fire to do this, but the most effective substance was believed to be pig's blood.

Many newborn babies did not survive after they were born. When a baby was born, the father of the house would decide whether it should live or die. Boys had a better chance because they would keep the family name alive. Girls were considered less valuable and fewer were allowed to survive. In fact, some historians believe as many as one in five newborn girls was left to die.

In ancient Greece life was good for the rich. They did not have to work hard and had a say in how their city was run. This meant, of course, that the rich families did all they could to get power and hold on to it. For the poor, life was a struggle. For the slaves, life could be sheer misery.

Chapter 2

Power Plays

A small number of rich and powerful families competed for power in ancient Greece. The infighting between these ruling families often ended in violence and bloodshed. The Alcmaeonid family was often involved in such battles. The family caused so much controversy that at one point they were **exiled** from the city, they refused to be kept away though and soon returned. The story of their exploits shows the dark side of politics at this time.

A bust of Pericles, a major political figure in Athens. Like many other important figures, he was part of a powerful family called the Alcmaeonids.

A Failed Rebellion

The Alcmaeonids earned their bad reputation because of events in 632 BCE. Cylon, an Athenian nobleman, tried to seize power in Athens by taking control of the Acropolis (the high ground that overlooked the city). However, he and his supporters became trapped on the Acropolis in a **siege**. Cylon and his brother escaped, but the rest were stuck in the Temple of Athena, patron goddess of the city. The temple was seen as a holy place and no one would attack them while they stayed there. However, they soon ran short of food and water.

Megacles was a member of the Alcmaeonid family. He was convicted of killing Cylon and exiled from the city, along with his family.

The rulers, known as archons, promised them a fair trial if they surrendered. The major archon, Megacles, was a member of the Alcmaeonid family. The plotters didn't trust him. They agreed to leave the temple, but to keep Athena's protection they tied a thread to a statue of the goddess as they emerged.

Some versions of the story say that the statue toppled over when they came out of the temple. Others say that the thread snapped. Either way, Megacles and his men stoned Cylon's supporters to death.

Banished

Megacles had broken a promise and attacked people under the protection of a goddess. In ancient Greece, entire families were punished if one of their members was convicted of a serious crime. The Alcmaeonids were exiled from the city. The bodies of their dead **ancestors** were dug up and buried outside the city walls. The family was cursed.

They returned, however, to join forces with a tyrant called Peisistratus. He had taken power using a clever trick in about 560 BCE. He had been a popular general but had little political power. In a cunning plot to gain power, he wounded himself and his mules to make

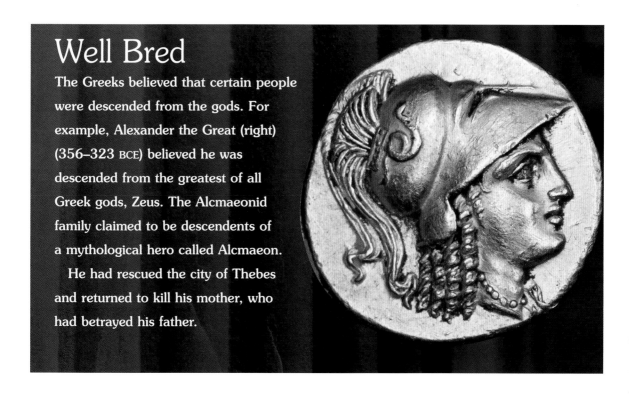

Well Bred

The Greeks believed that certain people were descended from the gods. For example, Alexander the Great (right) (356–323 BCE) believed he was descended from the greatest of all Greek gods, Zeus. The Alcmaeonid family claimed to be descendents of a mythological hero called Alcmaeon.

He had rescued the city of Thebes and returned to kill his mother, who had betrayed his father.

it look as if they had been attacked in the city. He entered the public square covered in blood. He claimed he had been set upon by enemies and needed to be given a team of bodyguards. He was the best military leader the city had, so citizens agreed to his request.

But now that Peisistratus had his own armed force, he used it to take over as ruler. Peisistratus used **bribery** and threats to persuade the voters to cast their ballots for his friends, ensuring his position as ruler.

Alliance

After a few years, Megacles's grandson, who went by the same name, got rid of Peisistratus and tried to rule himself. But he found he too could not hold on to power. So he went back to Peisistratus and persuaded him to marry his daughter.

Peisistratus used trickery and bribery to seize power in ancient Athens.

As goddess of wisdom and war, Athena was a powerful symbol. Peisistratus used a woman in her image to help him take control of the city.

Now they had an **alliance**. Between them they came up with another plot to persuade the public that Peisistratus wasn't such a bad ruler after all.

They found a tall, attractive woman and dressed her to look like the goddess Athena. Peisistratus and the woman rode into Athens on a **chariot** crying "Athenians! Give a warm welcome to Peisistratus! Athena has honored him above all other men and is herself bringing him back to her own acropolis!"

The trick worked and Peisistratus was back in power, this time with the support of the Alcmaeonid family. But yet again they argued. Peisistratus refused to have children with his Alcmaeonid bride because he thought they would be a threat to his sons from his first marriage. The Alcmaeonid family threw Peisistratus into exile again in 550 BCE.

Back in Power

Peisistratus cleverly came up with another strategy to regain his power. He gathered support from two other powerful city-states and gathered a large army to the north of Athens. A decade after being sent into exile, he returned to Athens, seized power, and ruled for another thirteen years. He in turn sent the Alcmaeonids into exile yet again and when he died his son Hippias took the throne.

Flowers and Daggers

In 514 BCE two men, Harmodios and Aristogeiton, plotted to kill Peisistratus and his brother Hipparchus to make way for a new tyrant. The plan was to stab them with daggers hidden in the floral displays at the Panathenaic Games. The scheme was all set when they saw one of their fellow conspirators chatting with Hippias. Fearing that they had been betrayed, they grabbed their weapons and quickly finished off Hipparchus. Harmodios was immediately killed by a guard and Aristogeiton was captured. Hippias tortured Aristogeiton until he revealed the names of the other plotters. Aristogeiton said he would tell the truth only if Hippias shook his hand to guarantee his safety. As they did this, Aristogeiton taunted the tyrant for shaking the hand of his own brother's murderer. Hippias then killed Aristogeiton.

Harmodios and Aristogeiton seized daggers hidden in flower displays to kill Hipparchus, brother of the tyrant Peisistratus, in a bid to end his rule.

Chapter 3

Written in Blood

Politics and laws in early Athens were not considered civilized compared to those of today. For example, in ancient Greece a fair punishment for stealing an apple was death.

With no police force and no set of laws, getting justice in ancient Greece was difficult. Families tended to take the law into their own hands if someone wronged them. The family that had been attacked would want revenge in retaliation. As a result, the killing of one person would often lead to the deaths of many more as each family avenged the latest death.

In ancient Athens, the defendant and the accuser were required to present their case before a jury of citizens. A government official convened the courts, but all final verdicts were left to the jury.

Draconian Law

In around 620 BCE a Greek nobleman named Draco was asked to write all the Athenian laws. This way, everybody would have an agreed set of rules to live by. The laws were posted in the city for all to read.

It was very important for people to know the laws because they were incredibly harsh. Draco believed that any theft was wrong, and that criminals should be killed. Draco's laws were very brutal.

Draco, a Greek nobleman, created a very harsh legal code for Athens.

Stone Dead

The Greeks approved of Draco's laws because they brought order to society. Sometimes they took the law too far though. There is a story of a statue that was taken to court and charged with a crime. A statue of the famous athlete Theagenes was erected on the island of Thasos. One of Theagenes' rivals was so jealous of him he flogged the statue every night. After a few evenings, the statue fell over and crushed the jealous rival to death.

The victim's sons took the statue to court for murder and the statue was convicted. The statue was thrown into the sea to "drown" as punishment.

Hats off to Him

Little is known about Draco, including how he died. One legend says that his life ended in a very strange way. He went to the theater and the audience, who approved of the work that he did in Greece, showed their admiration in the traditional way by throwing their clothes on his head. He was showered with so many hats, shirts, and cloaks that he became trapped under them and suffocated to death. He was buried in the theater.

Severe Punishments

Crime in ancient Greece was punished severely. Criminals were executed if found guilty of murder, theft, kidnapping, or temple robbing. In very serious cases such as treason and robbing a tomb, the condemned person was refused burial. The ancient Greeks believed people could not get into heaven unless they had a formal burial. The accused would be hurled off a cliff and left to rot in a rocky gully below the Acropolis. The Greeks believed that the unburied dead would spend eternity on the banks of the Styx River, which separated Earth from the Underworld. Eventually, Draco's laws were changed so that the punishments were not as severe, unless the offense was murder.

The Brazen Bull

In the Greek city-state of Sicily another punishment took place in the brazen bull. Offenders were placed inside the hollow of a bronze bull statue. A fire was lit underneath it until the metal glowed yellow while the victim was baked alive inside. The victim's howls of agony were amplified through pipes built into the bull's horns.

Famous Victim

The most famous victim of Greek justice was also one of its greatest and most notable thinkers and teachers, Socrates. He loved to argue about ideas because he

Socrates (second on the left) was one of the greatest teachers and thinkers of all time.

Justice in the End

Phalaris, the tyrant of Acragas, ordered the creation of the brazen bull. He demanded that the horn sound system be tested on the inventor, Perillos, himself. After Perillos was locked in, a fire was set so Phalaris could hear his screams amplified through the horns. Just before Perillos was about to perish, Phalaris opened the door and let him out. Perillos thought he would receive a reward for his invention, but after freeing him from the bull, Phalaris threw Perillos from the top of a hill, murdering him. When Phalaris was finally overthrown in 554 BCE he was stuffed into the bull and cooked alive, just like his unfortunate victims.

believed arguments led to greater understanding. Sometimes others were not grateful to be shown the faults in their thinking and did not like it when Socrates pointed them out.

Socrates was a popular teacher but some felt he did not show enough respect for tradition. In 399 BCE Socrates' enemies used the law to kill him. He was charged with not respecting the gods and with damaging the minds of young people.

At his trial he refused to use the tactics other accused people employed to get sympathy, such as crying, pleading for mercy, and showing the jury his children. Instead he carried on his arguments. When asked to suggest his own punishment he said he should be paid a wage by the government and receive free dinners for life because of the service he gave the city.

Fines and Flogging

A set of ancient Greek laws from around 250 BCE show how punishments were much tougher for slaves than for free men. A free man who threatened or struck another person was fined 100 drachmas. A slave's punishment for the same crime was one hundred lashes. If a master wanted to spare his slave he had to pay 200 drachmas.

Poisoned Potion

Socrates was found guilty and given what was thought to be the kindest method of execution at that time. He was ordered to drink a mixture of the poisonous herb hemlock. This herb shuts down the systems of the body until death sets in. He could have escaped into exile, but Socrates took the punishment. It was a painful, but quick death.

Socrates was found guilty of his "crimes" and forced to kill himself.

Chapter 4

War Makers

The ancient Greeks were usually involved in conflicts. For much of the time they were planning, preparing, or recovering from a war. The thirty city-states of ancient Greece did not trust one another. The smaller city-states knew they could not win a war on their own, so they would make alliances with other small states. Or, they would make an alliance with a larger city-state, such as Athens or **Sparta**, for protection. These alliances were often the cause of wars.

There were also threats from outside the empire, especially from the Persians. Often, the city-states would unite against these outsiders. Sometimes one city-state would betray the others and join the Persians in the hope of winning more lands.

The Greek forces were heavily outnumbered by Persian attackers at the Battle of Marathon. But they were better equipped and organized and were able to slaughter more than six thousand of their enemies.

Fighting Talk

The Greeks greatly admired fighters. Many of the characters in Greek **mythology** are great warriors. These ancient heroes set the standard for fighting. For example, the *Iliad* by Homer tells the story of the Trojan War. One brave warrior, Patroclus, "kept on sweeping in, hacking them down, making them pay the price for Argives slaughtered. There Pronus was first to fall—a glint of the spear and Patroclus tore his chest left bare by the shield-rim, loosed his knees, and the man went crashing down."

Tactics

The Greeks did not have full-time armies. In times of war every male was expected to fight. However, they did not fight as individuals. Greek generals worked out better ways to fight

Patroclus was a legendary fighter from Greek mythology. Real-life Greek warriors were encouraged to emulate his bravery.

Wall of Mistrust

In 479 BCE Athens defeated a Persian attack and was going to rebuild its city walls. Its rival Sparta argued that a walled city could become a base for the Persians if they returned and believed no city should have walls. The Athenians assumed that the Spartans wanted to keep Athens weak so that they could attack it some time in the future.

than simply charging at the enemy. Starting in about 700 BCE, soldiers, known as **hoplites**, started to fight in line formation, standing shoulder to shoulder. Each man was protected by his own large bronze-covered shield on his left arm. To his right the shield of the next soldier protected his right side. This formation was called the **phalanx**. When a phalanx moved forward it created a wall of shields coming at the enemy.

The hoplites were well equipped and worked together in a formation called a phalanx that was very hard to defeat.

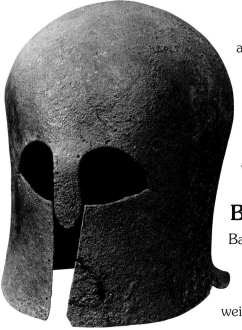

At the sound of a trumpet the phalanx would advance at a fast walk while the front row raised their 8-foot (2.5-m) spears. The walk would speed up to a jog as they tried to force their way through the enemy formation to split the opposing army. Once the enemy formation was divided, the hoplites picked the weaker section and attacked them with short swords.

Blood and Dust

Battles were noisy with blaring trumpets, shouting, and the cries of the wounded. The hoplites could not see or move well through their heavy armor, which weighed about 70 pounds (32 kilograms). Battlefields were bloody from spear and sword wounds.

Bronze helmets were often taken from the bodies of defeated enemies along with the rest of their armor.

Sometimes the battle was short and would be over in less than an hour. But there were times when they lasted far longer and many died horrible deaths in the mud and dust.

For example, in 394 BCE, four thousand men died during a massive battle between the allies of Athens and Sparta. Some battles were very one-sided. In 499 BCE, the Athenians defeated the Persians with the loss of only 192 men. They killed 6,400 Persians in the battle. Most of the dead were later cremated on the battlefield.

New Weapons

Gradually other weapons and types of warriors were introduced. Lightly armed soldiers with bows and arrows, slings, or javelins could move faster than the heavy,

Javelin-throwers were useful in battles because they could attack from a distance.

Dead or Alive

In 441 BCE, the Athenians beat the Mytilenaeans and debated how to treat their defeated enemy. They voted to kill all the men and sell the women and children as slaves. They then sent a boat to the Mytilenaeans with the message. However, the debate continued and they changed their minds. A second boat was sent to overtake the first with a new message. It arrived just as the death sentences were being announced. It was decided that only the ringleaders of the rebellion were to be executed, though this still amounted to about one thousand men being put to death.

slow hoplites. The javelin in particular was a vicious weapon that was thrown over long distances. This allowed the thrower to avoid getting anywhere near the swords and spears of the enemy. A flying javelin was powerful enough to pierce a solder straight through and kill him.

Cruel in Victory

Victorious Greeks were ruthless once a war was won. Enemy commanders were executed and their soldiers were slaughtered or made into slaves. They were often forced to work in the worst jobs, such as in quarries and mines. Others might be kept as hostages and used as a bargaining tool. Women and girls were also enslaved, while their villages were looted and burned.

Street Fighters

A civil war that was fought with hand-to-hand combat took place in 427 BCE in Corcyra. Women took part in the battle throwing tiles at one another. It became a bloodbath and some people chose to kill themselves rather than face an even worse death at the hands of an enemy. The Greek historian Thucydides described a dark scene where people "hanged themselves from trees.

Athenian historian Thucydides wrote to a great extent about Greek fighting methods.

Others killed themselves in any way they could…. Fathers killed their sons. People were dragged from the temples and slaughtered in front of them; some were even walled up in the temple of Dionysus and left to die."

Sieges

Battles were not the only form of warfare in ancient Greece. At times, cities were held under siege. In a siege soldiers would stop food from getting into a city and wait for those inside the walls to starve and surrender. However, some formidable siege weapons were developed to force those within the city walls to surrender more quickly. One was the siege tower. Standing 140 feet (43 m) high (about the height of a nine-story building), it was equipped with catapults manned by hundreds of men. It took a team of several thousand to pull it. It would be used to fire missiles down over the protecting walls, and, if it got close enough, as a structure from which attackers could enter the city.

Another siege weapon was the belly shooter, which was a type of giant bow that could fire objects other than arrows. It was given this name because a soldier rested the bow part against his stomach and pushed forward to set the weapon. It could fire rocks and other projectiles about 250 yards (230 m) like missiles over the walls of the city under siege.

Sieges were difficult because it could take a very long time for the inhabitants of a city to surrender. This meant the army outside the walls would be forced to camp there for months or even years. Armies in such situations suffered great hardship.

Scary Scythians

The enemies every ancient Greek feared the most were the Scythians. The Greek historian Herodotus wrote of how they treated their defeated victims: "The Scythian soldier scrapes the scalp clean of flesh and, softening it by rubbing it between the hands, uses it . . . as a napkin. The Scyth is proud of these scalps and hangs them from his bridle rein." Scythians were also known for their habit of cutting off the heads of slain enemies and making drinking cups from their skulls.

Siege towers were massive structures that allowed weapons to be fired into cities and for soldiers to climb over protective walls.

Often these armies caught deadly diseases, such as the plague. Some sieges were simply given up after years of waiting.

Naval Warfare

In 483 BCE, Athens made an important decision. In order to gain greater status, the city decided it needed to build a fleet of ships and become a naval power. This would enable Athens to hold the supreme position in ancient Greece.

The belly shooter was like a large cross-bow. It was held against the user's belly when being fired.

The Athenians developed ships called *triremes*, which were boats with three banks of oars. Triremes were about 170 feet (52 m) long and were manned by 170 rowers plus a small crew and some soldiers. They were designed to be fast and easy to steer. This was

War Elephants

When Alexander the Great fought in India in 327 BCE he came across a new battle strategy involving the use of elephants. The opposing general Porus put two hundred of the mighty beasts on his front line to frighten the Greek horses. However, the strategy failed. The noise of the battle terrified the elephants. They stampeded in fear, trampling many of Porus' own men.

Shocking Surrender Terms

In 440 BCE the Athenians besieged Samos for nine months before the city yielded. The surrender terms were that the Samians had to pull down their own walls, hand over people to be hostages, destroy their own fleet, and pay damages. This wasn't enough for the Greek leader Pericles though. He tied the Samian commanders to posts in the marketplace and left them there for ten days. Then he gave orders for their heads to be bashed in with clubs and their bodies left on the ground to rot.

important because the basic tactic of sea warfare at that time was simply ramming the enemy craft in order to break it up so that it sank or at least could not sail properly. If that didn't work, soldiers boarded the enemy ship and fought in hand-to-hand combat.

Fighting at sea was dangerous because of the high risk of drowning if the ship was sunk. When the Athenian and Spartan fleets met in 406 BCE, thirteen Athenian ships went down and almost the same number was damaged and unable to help those in the sea. About three thousand Athenians went to a watery grave.

Triremes, the warships of ancient Greece, were able to transport large numbers of troops and were designed to ram enemy craft.

Chapter 5

The Spartans

The Athenians were the main power in ancient Greece, but they had a major rival—the Spartans. The war-hungry lifestyle of the Spartans made the Athenians look very meek in comparison. When Spartan men went to war their women would hand them their shields and say "With this, or upon this." This saying meant that they should only return from the war having won (with the shield raised in victory) or dead (being carried on it).

War and pride were everything to the Spartans. Men did nothing but prepare for battle. Children were brought up to be tough so they could survive warfare.

Spartan society was set up for war. To return from a battle defeated meant shame for your family. Soldiers were expected to fight to the end for the Spartan cause.

Nasty Neighbor

Sparta was located inland in what is now southern mainland Greece. Other city-states were built along the coast. Their inhabitants traveled the seas looking for new lands and people to conquer and enslave. Sparta established armies and fought with its neighbors instead. As Sparta's king, Agesilaus, commander of the army from 404–371 BCE, said, "The walls of Sparta were its young men and its borders the points of their spears." At its peak, Sparta controlled an empire of more than 3,000 square miles (4,800 square kilometers), which was about three times the size of the city-state of Athens.

The men of Sparta were free from all duties except fighting. They were trained to obey at all times, and were the only full-time soldiers in ancient Greece. The very sight of row upon row of Spartan hoplites was terrifying. The Spartans were famous for never giving up—those who lost their swords fought on with their fists and their teeth.

The Spartan king Agesilaus was once asked how big Sparta could be. He waved his spear and said "As far as this can reach."

Happy in Grief

Only men who had perished in battle (and women who died in childbirth) were given the honor of a tombstone in Sparta, unlike the rest of the Greek world. The relatives of the dead would smile with pride, while those of the survivors were gloomy with shame. One mother met her son on his return from a battle where everyone else had died. She screamed, "So they sent you to tell us the bad news?" She picked up a tile and hurled it at him, striking him dead.

The gravest sin in Sparta was if a soldier came back without his shield. It was assumed he had thrown it down and run away from the enemy. Soldiers who returned from a lost battle alive were called cowards. Such soldiers were forced to wear cloaks with colored patches. They were

Big Power

Sparta became important after it formed the major part of the Greek forces in the Persian Wars, which lasted from 499–450 BCE. From 431–404 BCE Sparta challenged Athens in the Peloponnesian War. However, after that Sparta started to run out of men because so many were killed fighting for their city-state that it could not maintain its male population.

only allowed to shave off half of their beards. They could not hold public office and it was unlikely that any woman would marry them.

State Property

Newborn babies were seen as the property of the state, not of their parents. It was against the law to bring up a handicapped or very sickly child. Babies were checked carefully for

Young Spartan men train before a crowd of onlookers. Spartan men began their training at the age of seven and continued until they were thirty.

At the Battle of Thermopylae in 480 BCE, a small force led by the Spartans blocked the path of a huge Persian army for days before being slaughtered.

signs of weakness at birth. If they failed the test their father was told to leave them at the bottom of Mount Taygetos, the highest mountain in Spartan lands.

Babies who were allowed to live were not taught to read and write as they grew up. Instead, they were taught to survive in the toughest possible conditions. Boys were taken away from their family at the age of six. They were brought up in schools where they were whipped for the tiniest wrongdoing. They were never given enough food and were encouraged to steal to get more to eat. If caught, they were punished with the whip not for stealing but for allowing themselves to get captured. At the age of fourteen boys were abandoned for a month in the countryside with no food. This forced them to learn to hunt and survive in the wild .

Women had a higher status in Sparta than elsewhere in the Greek world. They could own their own property, marry at an older age, and look after their husband's interests while he was away fighting. Women were respected because they could give birth to the new soldiers.

The Helots

The people who had the toughest time in Sparta were the **helots**. This was a group of people who included neighboring tribes and captured prisoners who had been forced to act as slaves to the Spartans. They were different than slaves in the rest of the Greek world because they belonged to the state, not to individual owners. They wore uniforms of simple clothing made from animal skins and leather caps.

Helots had no legal rights and could be killed without trial if they were suspected of wrongdoing. Every year in the fall the Spartans held the Crypteia, a killing festival. Young men were sent into the countryside with instructions to murder any helot they came across. This type of military training also helped to keep the helots frightened and obedient.

The Spartans were proud of their ability to withstand pain. One of their kings, Cleomenes, whose reign began in about 520 BCE, took his pride a bit too far. He plotted against a fellow king and was put in prison in about 489 BCE. He borrowed a knife and began to cut his own body, working up from his shins. By the time he had got as far as slicing into his own belly he was dead.

Fox Cub

A boy stole a fox cub and hid it under his cloak. He was caught by the farmer who owned the land. The man asked the boy what he was doing but he didn't reply. Suddenly he fell down dead. The hidden animal had eaten his insides, yet he had not cried out in pain in case he was found out: death was better than being branded a criminal.

Walled In

Pausanias was a Spartan general who learned the hard way not to plot against his own people. Although he won battles against the Persians, he was suspected of **treachery** and brought back to Sparta. He sent a messenger, Argibius, with a letter to the Persian general Artabazus.

Rebels

Helots outnumbered the citizens of Sparta by about five to one, and sometimes they rebelled. To prevent such revolts, in 424 BCE, the Spartans announced that the bravest helots were to be given their freedom. Two thousand were chosen and crowned. Then they were killed because the Spartans judged they were the greatest threat to the state.

Argibius realized as he traveled that all the other messengers from Pausanias were dead. He opened the letter and found it instructed Artabazus to kill him to make sure he did not tell anyone else about the message. So Argibius went to the Spartan magistrates who now had evidence that Pausanias was up to no good. They decided to arrest him.

When the authorities came for Pausanias he was rushed to the safety of the temple of Athena where he could not be touched. The Spartans kept their honor and did not touch

The Spartan general Pausanias was suspected of plotting with the Persians. He was walled up in a temple and left to die.

The defeat of the Spartans at the Battle of Leuctra was a major shock in the Greek world as they were always expected to win on the battlefield.

him. Instead they bricked up the doors and walled him up inside. The first brick was laid by his own mother, who was ashamed of her son's betrayal. Pausanias starved to death inside.

The Spartans fought so many wars with such high loss of life that they started to run out of men. Sparta began to hire **mercenaries** to fight for them. In 379 BCE they were defeated by the Thebans at the Battle of Leuctra and lost one thousand men. Even the Spartans could not take such an onslaught. Sparta never recovered.

Chapter 6

Gory Games

The Greeks loved sports but the early games were a long way from today's **Olympic** ideal of peaceful competition. In fact, competitors could be killed by taking part in some of the events of the early Olympics. Many of the events held at the Olympic Games were based on military training exercises. Soldiers had to be able to run fast and to throw and fight well. For example, the final event was a two-lap race, but at the ancient Greek Olympics, the runners had to wear full hoplite heavy armor and carry a shield.

It is not clear how the Olympic Games started, but they were closely linked with religion. They were held at the site of Olympus, home of the chief god, Zeus, so they are likely to have begun as part of a religious festival.

The victors at the Olympic Games became celebrities who were regarded as heroes just like top athletes of today.

Fire Starter

The first Olympics only had one event: a race. A priest would **sacrifice** an animal on the altar of a temple. Then the runners would race on a track around the temple, finishing in front of the altar. The winner of the race had the honor of lighting the fire on which the animal was to be cooked to be served to the gods and their worshippers.

Human Meat

The Greeks, who loved stories, had another far gorier version of how the Olympics began. According to myth, a man called Tantalus decided to see whether the gods really knew everything. He invited them to a meal at which he served up the body of his own son, Pelops. All the gods spotted the trick and refused to eat, except Demeter, who ate Pelops's shoulder. Tantalus was punished by being forced to live up to his neck in water under a fruit tree. However, whenever he tried to drink, the water drained away, and whenever he reached for the fruit, the winds lifted the branches out of his reach.

The gods brought Pelops back to life and he fell in love with Hippodamia, the daughter of Oenomaus, king of Pisa. This king was jealous of anyone who loved his daughter and would challenge them to a chariot race, which he fixed so that his opponents were killed.

Pelops set up the race at Mount Olympus (home of the chief god, Zeus). Before the race, however, Pelops switched the metal pins that held the king's chariot wheels in place with pins made of wax. During the race the wax

Tickets Please

Not everyone was welcome at the Olympic Games. Foreigners who did not speak Greek were banned. Women were not allowed to attend because Olympia was a place sacred to men.

Tantalus' punishment for tricking the gods was to spend eternity tempted by water he could never drink and fruit that he could never reach.

pins melted in the heat, the chariot crashed, and the king died. Pelops married Hippodamia and founded the Olympic Games to celebrate his victory.

Wheels of Death

The first Olympic Games on record took place in 776 BCE. They were held every four years from then on. One of the most spectacular events to watch was the chariot race. In this race, two-wheeled chariots were pulled by teams of four horses. They hurtled up and down a straight track twelve times. At each end they had to turn all the way around. This was extremely dangerous because the cart could easily overturn on the bumpy track. There was always the risk of sideways or head-on collisions with other racers as well.

The charioteers were required to tie the horses' reins around their bodies. If they fell, the running horses would drag them along the ground. The charioteer would be lucky to escape

Chariot races were extremely dangerous and the prize for winning went to the owner, not the rider.

with only an injury and not be killed. In one race at Delphi, not part of the Olympics, it was written that "forty drivers were laid low," meaning they were injured or killed.

The winner of the race was the chariot owner, not the driver. Owners could have more than one chariot in the race, and used the event to show off their wealth. This meant that their drivers could work as a team, deliberately crashing into rivals so that another of their owner's chariots could win.

More than Glory

It is often said that the athletes of ancient Greece only competed for the glory of victory and the privilege of wearing the crown of olive leaves. In fact, winners were rewarded with lifetime jobs in the army or politics. They were also guaranteed free meals for life and the type of fame that made them the celebrities of their time.

Boxing

Boxing matches took place between two fighters chosen at random. There was no attempt to match them by weight or height to make for a fair fight. The boxers didn't wear gloves but tied leather straps around

Boxing at the ancient Olympic Games was brutal and the fight continued until there was a clear winner—the last man standing.

Milo of Croton was famous throughout the ancient Greek world for his feats of strength and his numerous wins at Olympic Games.

their hands to protect them. There was no time limit on the length of the fight. It continued until one of them was knocked out or gave in. If the fight went on too long, the boxers could finish it by agreeing to punch each other undefended in a "punch out."

Cow Catcher

One of the greatest champions was Milo of Croton, who lived in the sixth century BCE. He won the wrestling competition at five Olympic Games in a row. For months before an event he would build up his strength by carrying a cow on his shoulders. Animals got their revenge in the end, though. When Milo tried to split open a tree with his bare hands, he became trapped. A pack of wolves set upon him and ate him.

Anything Goes

One event, called **pankration**, was extremely violent. Pankration was a mixture of wrestling and boxing. Only biting and gouging out your opponents eyes were banned. Otherwise you could do what you wanted. Injuries were inevitable and it was not uncommon for fights to end in death.

And the Winner is Dead

During a pankration event, a fighter called Arrichion was being held so tightly by his opponent that he could hardly breathe. He managed to grab the other man's foot and twisted it around so much that he dislocated his opponent's ankle. Unable to bear the pain, his opponent raised his hand to give up, just as Arrichion died of strangulation. Even though he died in the event, Arrichion was declared the winner because his opponent had surrendered first.

At the Nemean Games, which were held the year before and the year after the Olympic Games, Creugas and Damoxenos fought to a standstill. They drew tokens to decide who would hit the first blow in the "punch out." Creugas smashed his opponent full in the face but he took the blow. Then Damoxenos pushed his fingers under Creugas' ribs and used his sharp nails to tear out his guts and kill him. But Creugas was awarded the title because the referee judged that his vicious opponent had taken two blows rather than the single one he was allowed.

The first discuses were made of stone, but later bronze, iron, or lead were used.

Taking Part

"It's not the winning: it's the taking part that counts" is a popular saying. But this wasn't true in the Olympic Games of ancient Greece. For example, if one competitor won the first three events of the five-event pentathlon (discus, javelin, long jump, running, and wrestling) the contest was stopped because no one else could win.

Chapter 7

Dark Tales

We know from the wealth of mythological tales from ancient Greece that the Greeks loved telling stories. They created a huge library of myths, which they used to explain how the world was created, what happened in times long ago, and why people behave as they do. The myths are full of adventure, betrayal, and violence and are populated by a huge group of gods with special powers, led by Zeus. Greek mythology contains **prophecies**, promises, punishments, and petrifying monsters.

Zeus was the king of the Greek gods. He controlled the weather and punished those who displeased him by throwing thunderbolts.

Prophecies

When Oedipus, the mythical king of Thebes, was born his parents consulted an **oracle**. The oracle told his parents that Oedipus would one day kill his father and marry his mother.

Horrified, Oedipus's parents strapped his ankles together and asked a shepherd to abandon him on a mountain. The shepherd took pity on Oedipus and gave him to a family who raised him. One day when Oedipus had grown up he met a man who insulted him and killed one of his horses. Oedipus fought back and killed the stranger. Only later he discovered the man was his father. As time went on he met and married a woman who turned out to be his mother. She was horrified at their mistake and committed **suicide** while Oedipus blinded himself with needles and wandered the earth in shame until he died.

In another myth, a man called Pelias imprisoned his half-brother Aenos in order to become king. However, an oracle predicted that one of Pelias's relations would kill him and that he should beware of a man wearing only one sandal. Pelias put all his relatives to death apart from Aenos. When Aenos's wife had a child Pelias ordered it to be killed but instead the child was smuggled out of the palace. This child, called Jason, grew up. One day, Jason helped a goddess disguised as an old woman cross a river, losing his sandal in the mud.

Oedipus was so ashamed of his past that he blinded himself and wandered the earth in shame until he died.

On the other bank was Pelias. He told Jason he could be king only if he captured a golden fleece, which Pelias didn't think

Jason gathered a band of heroes called the Argonauts who shared in his adventures as they helped him in his quest to find the Golden Fleece.

The story of Theseus defeating the Minotaur may have its origins in the killing of human sacrifices on the island of Crete.

Jason could manage. Jason returned victorious after many adventures only to find Pelias had forced Aenos to commit suicide. In revenge, Jason's wife played a trick on Pelias' two daughters. She convinced the girls that she had a magic cauldron that made the old young again. The two daughters chopped up their father and cooked him in the pot thinking they would make him young again. With King Pelias dead, Jason was able to take the throne and become king.

Promises

Two broken promises have terrible results in the story of Theseus and the **Minotaur**. The Minotaur was a half-man, half-bull that lived in an underground maze in Crete. Groups of seven young men and women were sent to Crete as payment from Athens every year and fed to the Minotaur. One year Theseus vowed to save them. He agreed with his father that he would signal his success by flying a white sail from his ship on his return.

Oracles

The Greeks often consulted oracles who were supposed to be able to predict the future. The oracle at Corinth had built a secret tunnel under the altar. It was just big enough for him to crawl through until he could lie under the feet of the visitor. When he answered the questions of the visitor he spoke into a tube. This made it sound as if the gods were speaking.

The tale of the ten-year siege of Troy has many features of Greek wars: brutal killings, revenge, treachery, and tricks.

He traveled to Crete and met Princess Ariadne who fell in love with him and gave him a sword that would kill the beast and a ball of thread to unwind so he could find his way back out of the maze. In return he promised to marry her. He killed the monster and escaped with Ariadne. But soon he grew tired of her and abandoned her on another island. In punishment, the gods made him forget to put up the white sail. When his father saw the ship's black sail he threw himself off a cliff to his death. Theseus never forgave himself.

In the story of the ten-year siege of the city of Troy, the Greeks captured a Trojan scout

Truth or Myth?

There may be some truth in the story of human sacrifices on Crete. Three sites on the island have possible evidence of the ceremonial killing of people. At one the body of a young man who had been tied up before death has been found next to a bronze dagger. From the positions of other bodies, some people believe a sacrifice was taking place when an earthquake brought down the temple.

Hera was both wife and sister to Zeus and was cruel to any who offended her.

called Dolon. He agreed to tell them the secrets about the Trojan army in return for saving his life. They agreed to the deal, but after he gave the information they broke their side of the bargain and cut off his head.

Punishments

The Fields of Punishment were the ancient Greek version of hell. In myths the punishments are eternal—they last forever. For example, Prometheus stole fire from his cousin, Zeus, and gave it to a human. In punishment, Zeus chained Prometheus to a mountain where an eagle would constantly peck out his liver. Each night his liver grew back and the eagle would peck it out all over again the next day.

Sisyphus offended the gods with his trickery. In punishment he was forced to roll a huge rock up a steep hill. However, the rock would always roll back down the hill just before he reached the top. This meant Sisyphus was condemned to the eternal and frustrating job of pushing the rock back up the hill.

Hera, queen of the gods, grew tired of the constant chatter from her servant Echo. In punishment,

Medusa was a gorgon: a woman with living snakes for hair and with the power to turn all who saw her to stone.

she condemned Echo to only repeat what someone else said. Echo heard the vain Narcissus say "I love you" to his own reflection in a pool of water. She repeated what he had said and he stayed there gazing at himself until he died. Echo faded away until only her voice was left.

Petrifying Monsters

The beasts of Greek myths are truly the stuff of nightmares. There were the Harpies who had the faces of old women and the bodies of birds with long claws. The Cyclops were giants with one eye in the middle of their forehead. The Sphinx had the head of a woman and the body of a lion. She stopped travelers and asked them riddles. If they failed to answer correctly she strangled them with her serpent's tail and ate them. The most petrifying beast of them all was the snake-haired Medusa, who turned anyone who looked at her face into stone.

These myths are one of many wonderful legacies from ancient Greece, the civilized world with a dark history.

Glossary

Alliance
A merging of efforts or interests between people, families, states, or organizations.

Ancestor
One from whom a person is descended and who is usually more remote in the line of descent than a grandparent.

Bribery
Something, such as money or a favor, offered or given to a person in a position of trust to influence that person's views or conduct.

Chamber Pot
A portable container used in a bedroom as a toilet.

Chariot
A cart with two wheels pulled by horses.

City-state
A state that is based around an independent city.

Civilization
An advanced state of human society, where there is a high level of culture, science, industry, and government.

Colonies
Territories with ties to a parent state.

Democracy
A government by the people where citizens can vote.

Drachma
The unit of currency found in many ancient Greek city-states.

Exile
To be away from one's state or country, either by being threatened by death or imprisonment upon return or refused permission to return.

Gorgon
A female monster so horrible to look at that anyone who saw her died.

Helot
A slave in Sparta.

Hoplite
A Greek foot soldier, named after the hoplon, their round shield.

Mercenaries
Soldiers who were paid to work.

Minotaur
A mythical half man, half bull that lived in a maze under a palace in Crete.

Mythology
Traditional stories about gods and superheroes.

Olympic Games

A sporting competition begun in 776 BCE and held every four years.

Oracle

A kind of prophet who could foretell the future.

Pankration

A violent sport that combined boxing and wrestling.

Phalanx

A block of hoplites in battle.

Plague

A highly fatal infectious disease that is caused by bacteria. It is transmitted by the bite of a rat flea and causes high death rates.

Prophecy

A prediction of the future.

Sacrifice

Ritual killing of people or animals to please the gods.

Sanitation

The disposal of garbage and waste.

Siege

Surrounding and sometimes attacking a place.

Slave

Someone who is forced to work for no pay and has no rights. They are often held against their will.

Sparta

A city-state of ancient Greece in the Southeast Peloponnese.

Suicide

When someone takes their own life voluntarily.

Treachery

Betrayal of trust.

Trireme

A warship with three rows of oars on each side.

Typhus

An infectious disease transmitted to people by the bite of fleas, lice, etc., and characterized by fever, headache, and red spots on the skin.

Map of Ancient Greece

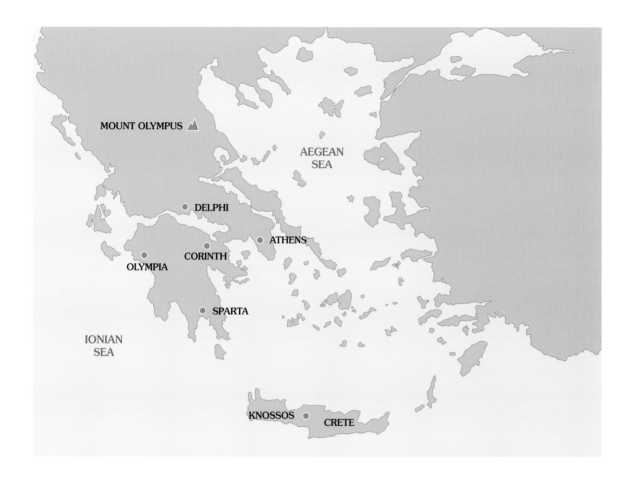

Ancient Greece was divided into three regions: the coast, the lowlands, and the mountains. Farming was difficult because of the rocky and uneven soil. Only 20 percent of the land could be farmed. The Greeks relied heavily on imports from other regions around the Mediterranean. The mountainous terrain made travel difficult which contributed to the formation of independant city-states throughout the region.

Find Out More

BOOKS

Hynson, Colin. *In Ancient Greece* (Men, Women & Children). London, UK: Hodder, Wayland, 2009.

Pearson, Anne. *Ancient Greece* (Eyewitness). New York: DK, 2007.

Roberts, Russ. *In Ancient Greece* (How'd They Do That? Lifestyle, Culture, Holidays). Hockessin, DE: Mitchell Lane Publishers, 2009.

WEBSITES

The Metropolitan Museum of Art
www.metmuseum.org/toah/ht/04/eusb/ht04eusb.htm

Minnesota State University
www.mnsu.edu/emuseum/prehistory/aegean/

University of Pennsylvania Museum of Archaeology and Anthropology
www.penn.museum/sites/Greek_World/index.html

About the Author

Sean Callery is a children's writer and teacher. He writes on a wide range of subjects including history, science, and the environment. He is also the author of *The Gem Guide to Dictactors*, the history section of the *Kingfisher Explore Encyclopedia,* and he contributed to *The Encyclopedia of Dinosaurs and other Prehistoric Animals.*

Index